PROVERBS

For

PROSPERITY

PROVERBS

For

PROSPERITY

Proverbs for Prosperity

First Edition / First Printing

Proverbs For Prosperity

Are you ready to prosper like never before? Do you want to walk in the prosperity that God has planned for you? Do you need a daily guide and reading plan to get you to a new place of prosperity? If you answered yes to any of these questions, this book is for you! *"Proverbs For Prosperity"* will take you on a journey to realize the blessings that God has ordained for you to walk in right now! Each day presents a personal scripture guide and reading plan to help you reach new heights of prosperity in your life! You will learn new ways to stay motivated and inspired. You will walk in a newness of joy, peace, contentment, abundance and prosperity as you complete each guide and reading plan in this book. Get ready to be blessed beyond what you can think or imagine.

Dedication

To my daddy, Anthony T. Pleasant, who was a perfect example to me of a real man. To my wife Kimberly, whom I love dearly. To My three children; Christian, Zion, and Nacara.

To my family, the Adams' in Memphis, Tennessee. I'm home now and complete!

To my New Zion Christian Church Family and Clark Atlanta University, thanks for allowing me to be used by God to bless others!

Humbly Yours in Christ,

Apostle Jamie T. Pleasant

Getting the most out of the
"Proverbs for Prosperity" book

Congratulations on purchasing this book! Get ready to achieve a new level of prosperity through your daily reading of this book. This book contains ten days of carefully selected proverbs that will guide you into a deeper revelation of God's plan for prospering you!

**²³ Buy truth, and do not sell it;
buy wisdom, instruction, and
understanding.**

Proverbs 23:23 (ESV)

Table of Contents

Table of Contents

Day One

Never Stop Learning

**[5] Let the wise hear and increase in learning,
and the one who understands obtain guidance,
Proverbs 1:5 (ESV)**

O ne of the biggest secrets to walking in sustainable prosperity is to never stop learning. In fact, if you say that you know it all, that is all that you will ever know.

If you say that you know it all, that is all that you will ever know.

We must always be avid learners that have an unquenchable desire to grow and explore new

17

things at all levels in our lives. Our new-found riches and blessings come from an undeniable passion and desire to explore new horizons daily. The secret to growing and expanding our lives is to become comfortable being uncomfortable! We must be willing to stretch ourselves in directions that we never imagined possible. When was the last time you changed jobs or took on a new leadership role in an area that you had no experience in? When was the last time you went rock climbing, ziplining or water rafting? Finally, when was the last time you took a course in something that you had no experience or knowledge of? It is when we explore new horizons, we expand our minds. When our minds expand, our thoughts expand. When our thoughts expand, our life expands. When our life expands, a new dimension of life opens up to us that brings a reality that we never imagined. The proverb says that wise people never stop learning. Wise people are wise because they are continuously expanding their minds and knowledge base. Wise people always want to expand their minds by learning new things. It is this increase in learning where prosperity lives. Prosperity is not a static entity. Prosperity is always evolving and expanding. Prosperity awaits those that are distensible. This is where Steve Jobs, Mark Zuckerberg, Jeff Bezos, Bill Gates and others dwell. They dwell in an ever-expanding atmosphere. They never stop learning. You and I can live this same type of life as we develop a mindset that says, we will always learn and never be afraid to go where we have never been before.

When we dare to go where we've never been before, we will get what we've never gotten before.

> *When we dare to go where we've never been before, we will get what we've never gotten before.*

Finally, the proverbs show us that a prosperous person accepts and embraces guidance in his/her life. When we become humble enough to know others that can share in our lives to bring growth to us, we then become set up to open the door of expansion and prosperity in areas that we never imagined. The secret to sustainable prosperity is to never stop learning, growing and exploring. Do something new! Try something that you view as being bigger than your ability to accomplish it! Grow! Expand! Achieve! Succeed! Prosperity is waiting on you.

Reflections & Guidance

Write below what you feel in your heart God Yahweh is saying to you in this chapter concerning prosperity as it relates to being a constant learner that appreciates guidance.

_____

_____

_____

_____

_____

_____

_____

_____

_____

_____

_____

_____

_____

_____

_____

_____

_____

_____

_____

_____

_____

_____

_____

_____

_____

Day Two

Divine Guidance Brings Peace and Joy to Our Souls

10 for wisdom will come into your heart, and knowledge will be pleasant to your soul;

Proverbs 2:10

Wisdom is when God Yahweh gives us the ability to apply His divine knowledge, experience, and understanding, to provide us with good sense and insight to everyday situations that might occur in our lives. God Yahweh knows all and sees all. He knows what has the potential to happen in our lives, whether good or bad every single day. He takes pleasure in allowing us the opportunity to prosper in all situations by sharing with us His divine

23

perspective about how we should act in our daily lives. The wisdom of God Yahweh is always willing, ready and present to guide us to a prosperous end regardless of any situation we may face. We can only receive His divine guidance when our hearts are open to His infilling of knowledge, wisdom and understanding. In other words, we must have an open and willing heart that is receptive to His promptings and movement in our innermost being. Our heart must be in tune with Him and open to his nudging at every turn in our lives. Wisdom begins in the heart, as it impregnates, flows and spreads throughout our entire being.

> *Wisdom begins in the heart, as it impregnates, flows and spreads throughout our entire being.*

Let's say that you just received some bad news about your personal finances. This disturbing news is that an unexpected bill just came up that will require you to pay one thousand dollars more than

24

you have at the moment. Your first natural reaction will probably be to become nervous, anxious and begin to worry about what to do next. However, if you focus and open your heart through prayer and petition to God Yahweh and let him know that you need His divine guidance in this matter, He will begin to immediately infuse you with His divine knowledge about how to handle this situation with grace and peace. The hardest thing for any of us to do is to focus on God when something has effectively disrupted our homeostasis. We tend to focus on the problem or issue and disregard God Yahweh supplying us with all the wisdom and knowledge that He is providing for us to remedy whatever we are going through. God Yahweh always has a plan for everything that we might experience in our lives. However, we must stay tuned in to Him by keeping our heart open to His voice and promptings in the middle of our most disruptive and challenging times we are experiencing. It is important to remember that instead of naturally reacting to a disruption in our life, we need to simply, spiritually respond.

> *Instead of naturally reacting to a disruption in our life, we need to simply spiritually respond.*

It's important to remember that the Spirit of God, who permanently resides in us, is stronger and more powerful than any natural event or circumstance that exists on the outside of us. Our aim is to tap into the Spirit of Wisdom in our heart and walk in the peace and joy of God Yahweh. Yes! We should expect peace and joy to be experienced at all times in our lives regardless of how disruptive and disturbing it may be in the physical realm. Jesus said, *"²⁷ Peace I leave with you; my peace I give to you. Not as the world gives do I give to you. Let not your hearts be troubled, neither let them be afraid"* *(John 14:27 ESV)*. It is important for us to realize that worldly peace is different from Divine peace. Worldly peace can be described as the absence of problems, issues and challenges that are based on external circumstances. Divine peace is internal and immutable. It can't be changed or altered because of the steady state of the Spirit of God to keep us in perfect peace during imperfect times. Life is not perfect, but God's peace is! Life is not perfect, but God's joy is! Life is not perfect, but God always is! Therefore, His divine guidance is always perfect in our lives. He wants us to bring every imperfect situation to Him and open up our hearts to His divine guidance that will refresh, restore and reignite our soul. When our soul receives His wisdom, a profound sense of joy, peace, love, happiness and confidence will permeate our entire being. We will experience an idyllic reality that is indescribable and life changing! Finally, it is important for us to open up our hearts and let wisdom, peace and joy flow endlessly throughout our entire being at all times and during all situations. God's wisdom is knocking on the door of your heart. Will you let His wisdom in? Is your heart open to receive divine guidance from God Yahweh? If you let Him and His wisdom in, your life will change to be one of eternal halcyon at new levels!

Reflections

Write below what you feel in your heart God Yahweh is saying to you in this chapter as it relates to prosperity and you walking in divine guidance to experience joy and peace in your entire being.

_____

_____

_____

_____

_____

_____

_____

_____

_____

_____

_____

_____

_____

_____

_____

_____

_____

_____

_____

_____

_____

_____

_____

Day Three

When You Give God Your Best,
You'll Get His Better

[9] **Honor the LORD with your wealth
and with the firstfruits of all your produce;** [10]
**then your barns will be filled with plenty,
and your vats will be bursting with wine.**
Proverbs 3:9-10

One of the most straightforward formulas to always prosper in all areas of your life, is to give God Yahweh your absolute best at all times! God Yahweh expects to receive the firstfruits of everything that we have.

31

Firstfruits is an Aramaic and Hebrew term that means, the very first and best of whatever you are given. Let's look at this a little deeper. Firstfruits means that we give to God Yahweh back the absolute best of everything he has ever given us. It means it is top of mind for us. That means when we give to God Yahweh, it is not an afterthought or what we do after we have done other things with our money, time and skill set. It means that the very first thing we do is give a minimum of ten percent of all of our income immediately whenever we get paid or receive money. It means that we take pride and joy knowing that before we pay a bill, buy something or invest our money, we give God Yahweh ten percent of all of our money upfront without hesitation or any contingency. This is one of the biggest barriers most people experience when it comes to prospering in all areas of their lives. Many people say that they honor God. However, true honoring of God Yahweh involves giving back to Him a minimum of ten percent off the top of all our earnings and financial increase in life. Most people miss the promise in scripture that comes with us honoring God Yahweh with our firstfruits. The promise from God is that He will fill us with more financial resources than we can store or ever need to use in our life. Take note that this overflow of blessings is not limited to financial resources. It means that there is an overflow of health, peace, joy, success and fulfillment in all areas of our lives as well. Prosperity is more than financial gain. Prosperity means that we have a fulfilled and satisfied life in all areas of our life! It also means that money by itself, doesn't bring us joy. It means that the wholeness of a meaningful life is constantly before us. We are always in a state of blissfulness that can't be shaken by any outside negative event that we may experience. It means that once we develop a mindset of giving God Yahweh our firstfruits, we will experience an overflow of prosperity in all aspects of our being. We will experience an overflow in joy, peace, love, forgiveness, hope, healing, confidence, ingenuity and excellent health. This overflow of prosperity shall never end and only flow stronger as we navigate the unending ebullience of our everyday life in the ubiety of God Yahweh! All that is required of us to put in motion this unending prosperous flow from God in all areas of our lives, is to give upfront and foremost, ten percent of all our financial increase. We must also not overlook

34

how we present firstfruits in other areas of our lives as well. For example, we should have a firstfruit mentality when it comes to our place of employment. We must have a mindset and work ethic to do and give our best at our place of employment. We should not work just to get a check. We should check to make sure that we are giving our best each and every day on our job.

> *We should not work just to get a check. We should check to make sure that we are giving our best each and every day on our job.*

We shouldn't be told what we should do in order to provide a better service to whomever we are working for. We should always first, think creatively about what we can do to make things better for who we have been called to serve. When we develop this mindset, we are setting ourselves up for the overflow of blessings in our lives. Are you ready to become rich? Are you ready to experience unending joy? Are you ready to walk in better health? Well then, begin to present your firstfruits in all areas of your life to God Yahweh. His words are true and powerful and will transform us into prosperous beings that others will look at and want to emulate. It's time to let your light shine. Shine your light in the dark places of others! Shine your light in the dark spaces of others' hearts! Shine your light in the dark places of people that have lost hope and have no vision of living a better life. Shine! Shine! Shine! As you reflect The Divine!

Reflections

Write below what you feel in your heart God is saying to you concerning how you can prosper in all areas of your life by giving Him your firstfruits.

_____

_____

_____

_____

_____

_____

_____

_____

_____

_____

Day Four

The Secret To Living A Long Life!

¹⁰ Hear, my son, and accept my words, that the years of your life may be many.

Proverbs 4:10

You and I can live an exceptionally long and prosperous life. God Yahweh uses Solomon to share with us that long life is in our grasp if we do a few things. We must first, not just read the word of God, but accept what we read. Acceptance of the word of God is more difficult than you might think. However, the key to releasing a wellspring of long life with vitality lies in the truth that we must accept the word of God

39

that we read and meditate on. In other words, we should never question or doubt what is written in the Bible. We should study it intensely and as we do; the Holy Spirit will lead us into the truth and consistency of God Yahweh's instruction for our lives. Most people think that man wrote the Bible. Some even say that Shakespeare wrote the Bible. Others say that William Tyndale authored a novel that we refer to as the Bible. However, we need not look outside of the Bible to find the truth concerning who the true author of the Bible is. It is written in 2 Timothy 3:16-17 that states, *All Scripture is breathed out by God and profitable for teaching, for reproof, for correction, and for training in righteousness, [17] that the man of God may be complete, equipped for every good work.* Let's look a little closer at this. Verse 16 says something very profound. It says that all scripture is breathed out by God. Do you see it? When God Yahweh breathes out, we inhale in. We inhale His being, life and substance. Yes! The more we inhale His divine breath from scripture, the more we live a life that is fulfilling and prosperous with good health. God never intended for man to die. He never intended for us to live a short life. Sin, through disobedience by Eve and Adam, did that. However, we can maximize our life span on earth as our spiritual life is already eternal and never ending. Now, let's revisit the meaning of 2 Timothy 3:16. This passage of scripture means that when we read and meditate on the word of God, He is breathing into us a divine inheritance! He is breathing into us a successful life. He is breathing into us a healthy, long lasting and fulfilling life. Never forget, that the breathing of God Yahweh into our being through scripture, is how we experience a divine and fulfilled life as we walk throughout the earth. The breath of God is where a transfer from Him is delivered to us that is more than a natural means to exist. It means that we are inhaling a supernatural and divine life as we partake of the Holy Scriptures. Now, let's go a little more in depth. In Genesis 2:7, it is written, *then the LORD God formed the man of dust from the ground and breathed into his nostrils the breath of life, and the man became a living creature.* Interestingly, it is only when God Yahweh breathed on Adam that he became a living creature. Also, notice that Adam existed when he was formed, but life did not take place until God Yahweh breathed into his nostrils. God Yahweh created us to do more than exist. He created us to live. He created us to be productive. He created us to fulfill His will on earth. Looking even more into the passage of scripture in Genesis 2:7, we see that Adam wasn't just a living being, he was a living creature. We must not overlook the revelation that the word creature comes from the word create, which we get the word creative. God Yahweh breathes life into us in order for us to create as well. We are to create by adding to this earth. We are to add to the lives of our families, friends and place of employment. When we can add to others' lives, we are doing kingdom work. When we do kingdom work, we are walking in the purpose that God created and assigned for us to do on earth.

> *When we do kingdom work, we are walking in the purpose that God created and assigned for us to do on earth.*

The more we are useful to God Yahweh by creating great life experiences for people we come into contact with, the more He will do to make sure we maximize our time here on earth. Are you making an impact in people's lives you come into contact with every day? Are you a game changer on your job? Are you the person that everyone wants to be around so that they can walk in the joy and success that they see in your life? If you answered no to the aforementioned questions, get on your knees and pray to God Yahweh and ask Him to anoint you with the ability to not just read and hear His word, but accept, understand and act on it as well. However, accepting God's word is not as easy as it sounds. That's where faith comes in. Do you believe that you can move mountains? If you do, then why haven't you moved any mountains yet?

Forget mountains. Have you moved any hills in your life lately? Have you moved annoying people out of your life? Have you removed the negative effect you experienced from disruptive circumstances in your life yet? Well, scripture tells us that nothing should shake us or set us back to the point that we become unproductive in this life. Philippians 4:4 says that we should be joyful always and reciprocate that joy daily. Notice that it is easier to read this passage of scripture than it is to accept it in the midst of a trying time. However, if we read the word enough and it becomes a part of us, we will begin to live just as the scripture dictates. We will begin to live a life that becomes unshakeable. Life on this earth can suck the life out of you. Worrying sucks the life out of you! Anxiety sucks the life out of you! Doubt sucks the life out of you! But, when we begin to accept the word of God Yahweh, He fills us with a divine anointing to overcome all disruptive circumstances in our lives. This is where your faith comes in. You must have faith that stands on the truth that you may not see relief in a certain situation immediately, but God's word will bring relief to you at the right time. Your faith must rely on the truth of the scripture and not the lie of what you are experiencing in your life. Truth and experiences are two different things. You might be experiencing pain in your body, but the truth is that God is healing you and has already healed you. You might be experiencing a layoff from your job, but the truth is that God Yahweh has already prepared a better job for you. He had to bless you through a lay off because you never would have left that job on your own. You may be

46

experiencing a shortage of money to pay all of your bills right now. However, the truth is, God Yahweh is moving on someone's heart to send you some money to help you meet your needs. Remember, if all you do is read Philippians 4:19 which states, *And my God will supply every need of yours according to his riches in glory in Christ Jesus,* but never act on it, you will continue to be in need of His resources. God Yahweh will not supply you with what you need if you don't supply Him with what He needs, which is faith!

> *God Yahweh will not supply you with what you need if you don't supply Him with what He needs, which is faith!*

We must constantly demonstrate to God that our faith is stronger than the fear that a circumstance is presenting to us. Our faith is the best evidence that

God is looking for to know that we accept His word. The more we grow in the acceptance and understanding of His word, the more of His life He gives us.

> *The more we grow in the acceptance and understanding of His word, the more of His life He gives us.*

John 10:10, shows us that, *The thief comes only to steal and kill and destroy. I came that they may have life and have it abundantly.* The thief here is not satan. The thief is anyone or anything that is influenced by satan with the sole purpose of placing burdens, lies and doubt in our lives that contradicts the truth that Christ wants us to live an abundant and fulfilled life. Terrible television shows that you watch, suck the life out of you. Derogatory music that you listen to, sucks the life out of you. Evil and divisive people that you surround yourself with, suck the life out of you. But, when we read, meditate and accept the word of God, we partake of the abundant life! An abundant life is a healthy life! An abundant life is a peaceful life! And yes, an abundant life allows us to prosper in everything that we do, wherever we are. Accept God's word! Accept His peace! Accept His joy! If we do these things, we will maximize our time on earth in good health along with an abundance of wealth. The secret to living a long life has been shared with us and we must accept it so we can possess it!

Reflections

Write below what you feel in your heart God is saying to you concerning you maximizing your life on earth as you walk in divine purpose.

_____

_____

_____

_____

_____

_____

_____

_____

_____

_____

Day Five

He's Watching To See If You
Are Ready For Your Blessing

**21 For a man's ways are before the eyes of the
LORD, and he ponders all his paths.**

Proverbs 5:21

O ne thing that we need to always remember is that we can't fool God Yahweh. He is all knowing and present everywhere at all times. He is even more in tune with us on an individual level as He constantly examines our hearts to see what we are thinking and planning. Jeremiah 17:10 states, *"I the LORD*

53

search the heart and test the mind, to give every man according to his ways, according to the fruit of his deeds." We can see that God Yahweh closely examines our ways and looks at our intent. He knows what our deepest thoughts and plans are. This is where we either prosper in what we pursue or fail. Even if we have achieved what we were going after but God Yahweh didn't bless it, the struggle, pain and turmoil are noticeable. It may even get to the point that we may end up depressed and exhausted beyond rejuvenation. The worst thing that can happen to us is to achieve something and not be fulfilled. There are many people in this world that have achieved what they think is success, just to experience inward turmoil and heartache. There are many people that you may look at and label them as being successful, only to be shocked when you read that they committed suicide or some other behavior that is not consistent with what they have accomplished in their life. The Bible talks about good success. That is what we are to desire and pursue. Good success is different from worldly success. Good success is God ordained success.

> *Good success is different from worldly success.*
> *Good success is God ordained success.*

God ordained success, is based on God examining our hearts and seeing that it lines up with His will with the intent of helping others and building His kingdom. God Yahweh looks very closely in our hearts and takes an imminent view of our pursuits and thoughts. He looks closely at the purpose of why we are pursuing something. For example, someone may want to acquire more wealth in the form of money. That person may think in their mind that if they become financially wealthy, they will give more money to their church, help those that are indigent and create generational wealth for their immediate family. Here is what God does when a person thinks these thoughts. He begins to search deep in the heart of the person and looks at his or her paths of action as time unfolds in the future. If God Yahweh sees that every time, temptation is presented to someone and he or she falls because of it, He immediately removes or delays His blessing from this person. He knows that what should be a blessing, will end up disastrous and place him or her in a worse situation than before this increase came in his or her life. When God examines our paths, which means he looks at all the options that will be presented to us and the response that we will make, He immediately takes action in our lives to make sure that we don't end up in an undesirable state that will distance our relationship with Him. You may be asking yourself, what can I do to make sure that whatever I am pursuing or desiring, will be blessed by God when he examines me? The answer is quite simple and straightforward. We should always communicate to God first what our desire, intent and pursuits are. Next, we should place those desires in His hands. Then, we should give it totally to Him and state clearly that we want His will to be done over our will. Also, we should wait for confirmation from God Yahweh as to what our next step should be, either to begin, suspend or abort our plan. It all depends on His divine guidance. We must remember that God sees and knows more than we will ever see or know. He is all knowing and all seeing and ever present in every dynamic of our lives!

> *God sees and knows more than*
> *we will ever see or know.*

We must never forget that His eye is on the sparrow, and He watches us even closer! He is watching to see if He can see His glory in what we do! He is watching to see if He can see His purpose for kingdom expansion in what we do! He is watching to see if He can see a positive testimony that we can provide to others about how His blessing has enriched our lives in a positive way! He is watching to see the fruit of the Holy Spirit in our lives when He blesses us. God blesses those, who bless others.

> *God blesses those, who bless others.*

God Yahweh blesses us to be a blessing to others. Our blessings are not for ourselves. Our blessings are to help others and show the world that God brings increase to those that live according to His word, ways and mandates. When we develop a mindset to bless others, share with others and enhance the lives of others, God moves in great ways to enrich us with the ability to prosper and live a long and fulfilled life. God Yahweh is willing and ready to bless us as long as we stay close to Him and never change the dynamic of our relationship with Him. Too many people leave God when they become wealthier. God Yahweh wants us to grow in our wealth as we grow in our relationship with Him.

> *God Yahweh wants us to grow in our wealth as we grow in our relationship with Him.*

Do you love God Yahweh? Do you have an unquenchable desire to be in His presence all the time? Do you love to pray with Him? Do you like to attend church? Do you serve in a ministry in your church? If you answered yes to all of the aforementioned questions, then you possess the relationship that God blesses! God Yahweh blesses those endlessly, that endlessly loves Him by being involved with His church, people and mission. God has a blessing for you. He is watching intensely to see if you are ready for His blessing! It's one thing for us to say we love God, and another thing to show Him how much we truly love Him!

Reflections

Write below what you feel in your heart God is saying to you to prepare you for His blessing.

_____

_____

_____

_____

_____

_____

_____

_____

_____

_____

_____

_____

_____

_____

_____

_____

_____

_____

_____

_____

_____

_____

_____

Day Six

**The Word Is The Light That
Guides You To Success!**

²³ **For the commandment is a lamp and the
teaching a light, and the reproofs of discipline
are the way of life,**
Proverbs 6:23

God Yahweh has ordained His word to guide and lead us in all areas of our lives. Please note that there is a distinction clearly explained about the word of God being a lamp as well as a light. Let's take a closer look at the word lamp. In this sense, as stated in Proverbs 6:23, the word lamp is a container that has a wick that is connected to oil that extends to the outer rim. In other words, the lamp contains all the internal pieces needed to be able to produce the desired effect, which is light. Light can only be emitted from the lamp if there is ample oil and a proper functioning wick. Take note that if there is no oil in the lamp, there will be no light emitted. Also, if there is oil in the lamp, but no wick, there will be no light emitted as well. Therefore, it is important that all the internal parts of the lamp must work properly in order for light to be produced. God Yahweh has designed His word to go inside of us and prepare us to be able to produce the light of success in the world. How much time are you spending consuming the word of God? Do you read the word of God every day? How many times each day do you read His word? The answer to these questions has a direct correlation with our ability to prosper in this life. Never forget that the word first must get on the inside of us in order to produce things on the outside of us!

> **The word first must get on the inside of us in order to produce things on the outside of us!**

The word of God Yahweh works on the inside to show us the path to success that He has planned for us. It's the internal working of the word that brings external blessings to us that we must never neglect in our daily walk of faith! We have been called according to scripture, to let our light shine, as we are the light of the world. God Yahweh created us to show unsaved and doubtful people what a great and fulfilled life that anyone can experience once they become saved and a citizen of the kingdom of God. The level of excellence that we display at work in everything we do, is the light that causes people to gravitate towards us, and ultimately Christ Jesus as well. The light that the word produces in our lives is not just for us, it is for others to come towards the light of salvation and a prosperous and peaceful place while they are still here on earth. If our lamp is empty, our lives will be empty as well. If our lamp is full but not functioning, our lives will be full of potential but won't be functioning to our fullest capability. We will only be existing and not living a joyful, adventurous and purposeful life. There are a lot of people full of oil, which is potential, and have never been able to burn with the excitement and passion of purpose in their lives. It is only when we begin to burn and emit the goodness of God Yahweh in our lives, that we truly walk in our God designed purpose. When people think of you, what are their thoughts? When people say things about you, what are they saying? When people describe your character, what narrative do they share? The way people answer all of these questions about you, are a testimony of the word of God's place in your life. Proverbs 6:23, goes on to say that not only is the word of God a commandment, that should be read, it must also teach us. When we approach the word and begin to learn from it, we will then experience change in our lives and will begin to illuminate a prosperous life to others. It's the teaching from the word of God that converts our potential into ability. Our ability then becomes our reality as we do what we have been taught.

> *It's the teaching from the word of God that converts our potential into ability. Our ability then becomes our reality as we do what we have been taught.*

Again, we must do more than simply read the word. We must learn from it. We must spend time in the word to let it instruct and show us its life-guiding ability. When we become students of the word of God, we open ourselves up to not just give light, but shine brightly. Our personality shines luminously! We become shining stars that others look up to, so that they can aspire to have a better life through Christ Jesus. We become shining stars to others in order that they will find their blessings in everyday life. The word of God transforms us into luminaries. A luminary is defined as one who is of prominence and possesses brilliant achievement.

When we give off our light, we are displaying our luminary endowment that God Yahweh wants the world to see. We have been created to achieve! We have been created to walk in prominence in everything that we do! Never forget that we don't simply achieve, but we brilliantly achieve! This means that we have unusual mental keenness. We can think on the spot. We can solve problems quickly and correctly. We can think of things and put them into motion, while others are still trying to figure out how to approach a situation. The word of God does all of this! God's word wants to guide us to a success level that we have never experienced. His word wants to guide us into prosperity which includes joy and peacefulness in all areas of our lives. Let's follow the guidance of God Yahweh's written word. Let's walk in the path that He has laid out for us to experience all the blessings in this life. Let's let the divine lamp of the word, which produces light, transform our lives for the betterment of the Kingdom of God.

Reflections

Write below what you feel in your heart God is saying to you to prepare you for His blessing.

_____

_____

_____

_____

_____

_____

_____

_____

_____

_____

Day Seven

See it Before it Happens

**[4] Say to wisdom, "You are my sister,"
and call insight your intimate friend,
Proverbs 7:4**

God Yahweh has given us the ability to see things before they happen. We can see remarkable things that He has planned for us before they manifest in our lives! We can also see demonic and detrimental things that satan wants to occur in our lives and avoid them. How can we see these things? How can we get prepared for the blessings of God Yahweh? How can we prepare to avoid or be victorious concerning demonic events in our lives? The answer and gift that He has given us is simply, Wisdom. Yes! Wisdom is the gift that continuously guides us through and around events in our lives. Notice that we must consider Wisdom as a sister. Why does the scripture refer to Wisdom as our sister? Well, a sister is someone that we should be able to confide in, trust and come to when we are most vulnerable about certain things. A sister is someone that cares about everyone in the family and will share great advice with anyone in need. Therefore, we are to regard Wisdom as a loving and caring sister. She will always be there to advise and watch out for us. The next gift that God Yahweh gives us is the ability to call out to insight. Insight is really foresight.

Insight is really foresight.

74

Insight allows us to get an understanding of things before they happen. Insight also allows us to manage challenging times much better. Insight allows us to look on the inside beneath the surface of what is occurring and respond accordingly in a Godly fashion. We can then go deep to the underlying causes of events before they happen. Additionally, we can examine those same underlying causes while they are taking place in our lives as well. For example, let's say someone walks up to you and starts telling you off or not treating you with respect. Instead of snapping back at them or getting into an argument or confrontation, insight can quickly show you what is the reason this person is treating you in this ungodly way. Now, instead of responding in a way they would expect you would by retaliating, insight might show you that someone was just very nasty to them and hurt their feelings. You would then become empathetic towards them and do everything to calm the situation. That is the power of what insight can do for us. Insight can save us from a lot of heartache and regret. Insight can help us reach out to people and help them understand why they are behaving in a certain way. We can do all of this without belittling them or hurting their feelings as well. Insight wants to have an intimate relationship with us as well. When we become intimate with insight and can recognize her voice, we will be able to share all of our fears, doubts and concerns with her, knowing that she will not use them against us, but help us overcome those concerns to become a better person. What is really great about insight is that we can look at what a great and prosperous future God Yahweh has in store for us. How wonderful it is to be able to see a blessing that God Yahweh has for us in the middle of a challenging time. For example, let's say you were just called in your boss's office and he begins to tell you that you are being laid off. However, at the very same time, insight is speaking to you and showing you the new business that you are going to start which will allow you to make more money and work flexible hours, which in turn, will allow you to spend more time with your family. Therefore, as the boss is telling you about your lay-off, you start smiling and begin experiencing peace, joy and renewed energy. That is the power of what insight can do for us! Isn't that wonderful? Insight gives us a peek at a prosperous future in what seems like a perilous time.

> *Insight gives us a peek at a prosperous future in what seems like a perilous time.*

How reassuring it is to know that we can see things before they happen as we develop an intimate relationship with Wisdom because we now see her as our loving and caring sister. The best way to show Insight that we are ready for a remarkably close relationship is to open up our hearts and express all of our concerns to her every single day. We need to talk to Insight in the morning, noon and nighttime. We need to talk to Wisdom before we go to sleep and before we get out of our bed in the morning. Also, we need to let Wisdom reveal Insight to us by listening more than anything. Listening is the key to hearing divine direction from God Yahweh. Sometimes, you should just quiet yourself and ask the Holy Spirit to begin to provide insight about what you will encounter for the day. Wisdom wants us to see things before they happen. Wisdom wants us to be able to see our blessing in the midst of a storm! Wisdom wants us to be able to steer away from harm before it comes near us! Wisdom wants us to be able to see hope in hopeless situations. Wisdom wants to help us grow our faith! Faith and the ability to see things before they manifest in our lives is the greatest ability God has given us. Our faith becomes unshakable when we can see a positive future before a negative situation shows itself to us.

> *Our faith becomes unshakable when we can see a positive future before a negative situation shows itself to us.*

We should always think of Wisdom as an intimate sister that is always willing to help us by sharing

God Yahweh's future plan for giving His best to us. We must look for insight. Therefore, we should strive to receive insight and walk in it with confidence at all times as we go to new levels of prosperity in our lives.

Reflections

Write below what you feel in your heart God is saying to prepare you for His blessing.

_____

_____

_____

_____

_____

_____

_____

_____

_____

_____

_____

_____

_____

_____

_____

_____

_____

_____

_____

_____

_____

_____

_____

_____

_____

Day Eight

The Voice of Wisdom Cries Out To Bless You

¹ Does not wisdom call?

Does not understanding raise her voice?

² On the heights beside the way,

at the crossroads she takes her stand;

³ beside the gates in front of the town,

at the entrance of the portals she cries aloud:

Proverbs 8:1-3

God Yahweh knows that wisdom is so important for us to possess, that He makes it easy for us to obtain it. If you look at Proverbs 8:1-3, you will see that Wisdom not only calls us, but it also raises its voice in order to make sure we are divinely guided by the Holy Spirit. This will be a revelation to many, but God Yahweh has designed Wisdom to shout out loudly to us. Most think that wisdom can only be obtained when we are in a quiet space or meditating. However, scripture clearly shows us that we are able to hear Divine wisdom during our busiest and noisiest of times. If you think about it for a moment, this makes sense. It is in our busiest and loudest moments that we are usually in a situation that requires us to make a sound decision. It is extremely hard to think judiciously in order to make prudent decisions during these chaotic moments. This is when Wisdom comes in and clears the path for us to think, say and do the right thing regardless of the situation. The scripture says that Wisdom *raises her voice*. The Hebrew word raise means to give, to cause to have, in the abstract sense or physical sense. Let's look at this a little deeper. The word raises means that God Yahweh has designed Wisdom in our lives as a gift to us that will cause us to receive it. In other words, Wisdom will always present itself to us in such a way that we can't deny it or question if it's genuine. As we grow in our relationship with the Holy Spirit, we will be able to sense when Wisdom is calling out to us in order for us to make Godly decisions and take right actions in our lives. The next word we need to focus on is the word, *cries*. Scripture says that Wisdom not only raises her voice but *cries aloud* to us. The Hebrew word *cries,* means to utter a sudden loud cry. Isn't it comforting to know that when we are trying to make sensible decisions and do the Godly thing, that Wisdom will come to us suddenly! That means instantaneously! That means, right when we need it! What a joy to know that God Yahweh has given us a Divine gift that is always there in the moment that we need it. When we ruminate on this scripture, we see that it is showing us how Wisdom is available when business is being conducted. This is the time when there are many options as well as distractions that we are facing from all angles. Imagine yourself buying a car and the salesperson and sales manager are talking to you at the same time and presenting so much information that you don't feel you have been given the proper time to think. We all know these high-pressure situations are designed by unethical people to not allow us to make sound decisions. Isn't it awesome to know that if we are ever faced with this kind of high-pressure sales tactic in the future, we can tune in to Wisdom that comes through the Holy Spirit and focus and make a great decision? How awesome that is for us! We must begin to tune in to the Wisdom of the Holy Spirit so that we can tune out the divisiveness of demonic distractions.

We must begin to tune in to the Wisdom of the Holy Spirit so that we can tune out the divisiveness of demonic distractions.

Please know that there is no way we can hear Divine Wisdom if we have not developed a personal relationship with Christ Jesus. We must spend time with Him in order to recognize His voice. If we can't recognize His voice in quiet

86

times. We will never be able to hear His voice in trying times.

> *If we can't recognize His voice in quiet times. We will never be able to hear His voice in trying times.*

We must practice being in the presence of Christ and God Yahweh as they speak through the Holy Spirit to us in all matters of our lives. Think for a moment about how many times you have made a decision and not clearly heard from God Yahweh. How many times have you said something and later knew that the words did not come out right? How many times have you done something and felt guilt, shame and pain because you know it was not a Godly act? We can minimize these mistakes by tuning in to the voice of Wisdom, who is the Holy Spirit that will guide us according to the direction

Of God Yahweh and Christ Jesus. You may say, but I have never heard from God Yahweh. I don't know what He sounds like. How will I know it's God Yahweh and not me? What does the Holy Spirit's voice sound like? Well, that is the tricky part that can only be remedied by practicing His presence in your life. One key thing to remember is that the Holy Spirit speaks to us, through us!

> *The Holy Spirit speaks to us, through us!*

This means that the majority of the time, Wisdom is trying to get to us instantaneously. In order to communicate with us, the Holy Spirit will sometimes speak through us in our minds through our inner voice, that we hear in our head. Did you get that? Okay, here is an example that might help you grasp that truth. Have you ever been driving and the light is green and something inside you says to slow down or stop? The light is green and you know that you have the right of way. However, something told you through your mind in your inner voice, to slow down. You slow down and sure enough, a car speeds through the red-light perpendicular to you. If you had not immediately responded to the inner voice in your head or heart that told you to slow down or stop, you would have been hit by the car that disobeyed the red traffic light. Well, that was the Holy Spirit speaking to you through you. A warning had to get to you in a moment's notice at the speed of sound and the fastest way for that to happen was for God Yahweh's message to reach you instantaneously. Another beautiful thing to note here is that you may have been experiencing numerous *"something told me"* moments in your life, even before you became a Christian. We must never forget that God Yahweh speaks to us even before we are Christians. It is only through the Holy Spirit we are able to hear the voice of God when Wisdom raises its voice and cries aloud to us in order to respond to the gospel that leads us to salvation. Also, never forget that the Holy Spirit raised His voice and cried out to many people in the old testament that weren't saved as well. How beautiful and wonderful it is to know that God Yahweh has given us a precious gift that will allow us to hear Him at any time.

Reflections

Write below what you feel in your heart God Yahweh is saying concerning you maximizing life on earth as you hear the Voice of Wisdom daily.

_____

_____

_____

_____

_____

_____

_____

_____

_____

_____

_____

_____

_____

_____

_____

_____

_____

_____

_____

_____

_____

_____

_____

_____

Day Nine

Mind Your Business

**7 Whoever corrects a scoffer gets
himself abuse, and he who reproves
a wicked man incurs injury.**
Proverbs 9:7

Sometimes it's best to not offer a suggestion
or advice to others. Scripture shows us that
only a certain type of person will respond
appropriately when we give them advice. We have
to be very sagacious when attempting to evaluate
whether our thoughts and advice to others will be
well received. The Holy Spirit doesn't want us
casting divine pearls among swine. We must

discern when, what, how and where to speak into other's lives. Proverbs 9:7 shows us that a scoffer is a person we should be very aware of when interacting with them. A scoffer is defined as someone that treats something that is shared with them with contempt. They will dislike you and ridicule you even before you are finished sharing your heart-felt thoughts with them. A scoffer doesn't value anyone's opinion or thoughts about him or herself. They think they know it all. Even more, they don't want to hear your thoughts or opinions as it is a direct threat to their ego and state of selfishness. What's worse is that, when we speak into a scoffer's life, we bring on ridicule and hate that God Yahweh didn't want us to experience. Scoffers welcome chaos, confusion and disharmony. They thrive off of disruption and

94

heated discussions. Their goal is to never reach a place of acceptance and unity. They want to increase turmoil and disharmony at all levels in an organization or group that they belong to. We must be very alert when we encounter others and quickly discern what type of person we are encountering. It must happen instantaneously! The longer we fail to make a proper evaluation of people that we encounter, the more we open ourselves up to be hurt and demeaned by them. Do you know that there are people that stay up all night and wake up early in the morning to plan how they can get you upset and unbalanced? Do you know that there are people who have studied you and look intently for a weakness in your personality in order for them to attack you? Do you know that people look to see where you are most vulnerable and open to

95

destruction? Yes! These captious people exist and they will bait you into a discussion where they know they can tear down your confidence, enthusiasm and positive mindset. The same way people plan to dismantle you, you should assemble a strategy of protection from them.

> *The same way people plan to dismantle you, you should assemble a strategy of protection from them.*

We must learn to avoid unnecessary attacks that others have carefully and strategically planned against us. Only wisdom can help us be victorious in these types of situations. We must learn to scan the environment that we are in and more importantly, scan the personalities that surround us.

> *We must learn to scan the environment that we are in and more importantly, scan the personalities that surround us.*

It takes a lot of practice to be able to discern at a moment's notice. However, the more you sharpen your senses and your spirit to your surroundings, the clearer you will see what others' motivations are towards you. It's important to know that Proverbs 9:7 is showing us that a huge part of our prosperity involves being in a peaceful state of mind, body and soul. It's always important to know if we are in a peaceful environment or not. It's more important to dictate and know where peace is and how to obtain it at all times. A scoffer doesn't know what peace is and will never welcome or accept it when offered it by others. Never forget that fact! If we are not careful to recognize and avoid a scoffer, we may even end up in a worse state by encountering a *"wicked"* person. The wicked person is one who is godless according to Proverbs 9:7. The wicked person has no divine or spiritual connection with truth and how to respond to Godly advice. When exposed to Godly wisdom, they reject, despise and renounce it, because it makes no earthly sense to them. The reason Godly advice will never make any sense to them is that they can't understand spiritual things with a natural mindset. 1 Corinthians 2:14, shows us that, *The natural person does not accept the things of the Spirit of God, for they are folly to him, and he is not able to understand them because they are spiritually discerned.* Not only do they not understand Godly principles and advice, but they also think it is foolish to adhere to any other teachings, truths and principles of God Yahweh! So then you may be asking, when should I interact and share my thoughts with others? Well, first of all, we must learn to mind our business. That is easier said than done. As Christians, we are called to help others and step in and lead them to Christ. The key thing to know here is that we are called to step in and help others and lead them to Christ when God shows us the way has been cleared by His Spirit for us to do our part in bringing His will to fruition in a person's life.

We are called to step in and help others and lead them to Christ when God shows us the way has been cleared by His Spirit for us to do our part in bringing His will to fruition in a person's life.

Never forget, that we must be tuned in to where and how God Yahweh is moving in someone's life and if it is our business according to God Yahweh's plan for us to be the one to help them grow in a certain situation. Only when we know God Yahweh's business, will we be able to properly mind our own.

> *Only when we know God Yahweh's business, will we be able to properly mind our own.*

In fact, if we never reach a level where Christ Jesus is sharing his business with us, we will always be open to unnecessary injury as stated in Proverbs 9:7, which includes insult, persecution, ridicule and pain. We must learn to be in tune with the Holy Spirit and God Yahweh's direction as we conduct everyday life. We will be able to save ourselves from demonic attacks that are designed to get and keep us off track of walking in prosperity, where peace is a huge part of our joy and happiness.

Reflections

Write below what you feel in your heart God is saying to you about maximizing your life on earth as you hear the Voice of Wisdom daily.

_____

_____

_____

_____

_____

_____

_____

_____

_____

_____

_____

_____

_____

_____

_____

_____

_____

_____

_____

_____

_____

_____

_____

_____

_____

Day Ten

Get Busy, Get Rich

⁴ A slack hand causes poverty,

but the hand of the diligent makes rich.

Proverbs 10:4

The best way to prosper financially and in other areas of your life, is to simply get busy. You must develop a mindset along with a work ethic to reach your financial and other prosperous goals. You must create movement through acting on what you want to achieve. Many people plan what they want, but it's the doing that makes a plan become a reality.

Many people plan what they want, but it's the doing that makes a plan become a reality.

Getting started and not stopping until you have achieved your goal for prosperity should be your mantra. Don't let anything, anyone or any challenging circumstance delay or stop your progress from manifesting. The key to achieving your goal of prosperity is simply to be diligent. A diligent individual is defined as a person who is characterized by care and perseverance in carrying out tasks. This means that you not only want to achieve your goal. You are fastidious and detailed during the entire process. You will take pride in every aspect of your own business. A diligent person also displays a persevering attitude. In other words, you are persistent in all you do regardless of the difficulties or delays outside of your control. For example, you may want to start a business. You then go to the bank to request a loan, only to be turned down. This is where your diligence must be displayed. You don't give up. You go to four additional banks and they all turn you down as well. You then decide that a bank loan might not be the best place for you to obtain the financial funding

104

you need to start your business. You then go to conferences and talk to investors and tell them about your business plans and all of them are not interested, but you still give each one your business plan and contact information. One day you get a call from one of the investors that you met. They invite you to lunch to discuss your business plan in detail. After three or four meetings, they offer you the funding you need to start your business. You look back and realize that you began this business idea three years earlier but never stopped working your plan by meeting people and telling them about what made your business special and primed to be successful. That is what being diligent is. It is about never giving up when others can't see what you believe about your plan. You must remember that the vision that God Yahweh gave you, is just that, a vision that only you can see. It is your responsibility to share your vision that is spiritual in a way that others can see it as you do. You may have to work two jobs while you wait for your vision to become a reality! You may have to sacrifice driving a new car now in order to wait on your vision to become a reality! You might have to delay wearing expensive clothes for a while, as you wait for your vision to become a reality! All of this is what being diligent entails. Look closely at Proverbs 10:4. It shows us that, *"the hand"*, makes rich. Notice it doesn't say that the hand makes one rich. In other words, the hand is the means for anyone that is willing to work to achieve a status in this lifetime of acquiring wealth. Your hand is capable of converting potential into reality.

> *Your hand is capable of converting potential into reality.*

Your hand has the power to change things that are spiritual into things that are material. How does this happen? It happens simply by the blessing of touch. That's right! When we touch something, we do more than just place our hand on it. When we touch something, there is an anointing that God Yahweh placed in us that is released and begins to manifest right in front of our eyes. Our God given vision must become flesh in order to dwell among us.

> *Our God given vision must become flesh in order to dwell among us.*

The touching and working of your hand are what transform dreams and visions into a living and useful reality. Never forget that in the beginning of this world, God Yahweh said and things happened. However, when it came to man, God Yahweh said let us make man into our image. He then formed man out of the dust with His hand and he came into existence. Notice that the scripture clearly says that when God Yahweh formed man with His hand, he merely existed. He still wasn't alive. Only after God Yahweh breathed into his nostrils did he become a living being. Never forget that your plan for prosperity requires that you speak it, work it and give it life.

> *Never forget that your plan for prosperity requires that you speak it, work it and give it life.*

When you are given a vision, write and then tell the right people about it! Next, work your vision by releasing the creative anointing that God Yahweh placed in your hand. Finally, as you are working on your plan, the breath that it takes for you to achieve each milestone of your plan will bring to life your pursuit of prosperity. Go for it! Speak it! Work it! Breathe on it! Watch your life change for the better! Prosper like you never have before! Prosper as God Yahweh wants you to! Prosper to contribute to society and those closest to you!

Reflections

Write below what you feel in your heart God is saying to you concerning the vision He has shown you about His plan for prosperity in your life.

_____

_____

_____

_____

_____

_____

_____

_____

_____

_____

Epilogue

One of the best ways to experience God's prosperity in your life is for you to give your life to Christ Jesus. Repeat these simple words and it will be a done deal. Repeat the following: Lord Christ Jesus as of this very moment, I accept you as Lord and Savior of my life. I now give my life to you, to be fashioned for your purpose and glory. Lord, all of these things that I have said, I honestly believe in my heart and have confessed with my mouth to you. Therefore, I know that I have received everlasting life based on the work that Christ has done and will continue to do in my life. Lord Christ, thank you for bringing me to this point of my life where I surrender my all to you. It is in the Holy Spirit through Christ Jesus, I say Amen.

Humbly Yours in Christ

Apostle Jannie T. Pleasant

**Book Dr. Jamie Pleasant for a
Speaking Engagement!**

For speaking engagements, please contact
Dr. Jamie T. Pleasant at
admin@newzionchristianchurch.org or
678.845.7055

About the Author

Apostle Jamie T. Pleasant, Ph.D., a modern-day polymath, is the founder and Chief Executive Pastor of New Zion Christian Church in Suwanee, Georgia. He currently serves as the Dean of Graduate Education at Clark Atlanta University. He is also a tenured Full Professor of Marketing at Clark Atlanta University's School of Business. Notably, he is the first faculty member in the university's history to be accepted into Mensa International, the world's largest and oldest high IQ society for individuals who have scored in the 98th percentile or above on an intelligence test. Dr. Pleasant is the first African American to graduate from the Georgia Institute of Technology (Georgia Tech) with a Ph.D. in Business Management with a concentration in Marketing, earning that degree in

August 1999. He is a 2016 recipient of the "Lifetime Achievement Award" from former President Barack Obama for volunteer and community service. He was awarded the "Game Changer" Educator Award by Reverend Jesse Jackson at the 2019 Rainbow PUSH International Convention. As a polyhistor, in addition to obtaining a doctorate degree in Business Management from the Georgia Institute of Technology, he holds a bachelor's degree in Physics from Benedict College in Columbia, South Carolina, Marketing Studies from Clemson University and an M.B.A. in Marketing from the very prestigious, Clark Atlanta University. Under his leadership, New Zion has grown from three members when it started in 1995 to well over 700 in weekly attendance, with a focus on economic and entrepreneurial development. God gave him the vision to establish a Biblically based economic development initiative for New Zion Christian Church. He remains at the pulse of the economic business sector. As a result, Apostle Pleasant is in constant demand to train, speak and teach others at all levels in ministry and the private sector about business and economic development across the country. He has created numerous innovative and industry leading ministerial, business and economic development classes and programs, along with SAT & PSAT prep courses for children ages 9-19. He founded The Financial Literacy Academy for Youth (FLAFY), where youth between the ages of 13-19 attend 12-week intense classes on financial money management principles. At the end of those 12 weeks, they receive a "Personal Finance" certificate of achievement. In 2015, he established The Young Leadership and Success Academy that teaches young people between the ages of 10-21 how to invest, make presentations and start and operate businesses. Other ministries he has pioneered include The Wealth Builders Investment Club (WBIC), which educates and allows members to actively invest in the stock market, along with the much-celebrated Institute of Entrepreneurship (IOE), where participants earn a certificate in entrepreneurship after three months of comprehensive training in all aspects of starting and owning a successful competitive business. The main goal and purpose of IOE is that each year one of the trained businesses will be awarded up to $10,000 startup money to ensure financial success. Apostle Pleasant has met with political officials such as former President Bill Clinton and Nelson Mandela. He has performed marriage ceremonies and counseled numerous celebrated personalities such as Usher Raymond, Terri J. Vaughn, and many others. Several gospel music artists have performed

117

at the church, including Tiff Joy. Each year, Apostle Pleasant conducts chapel services for Clemson University's football team and is a spiritual and personal friend to its two-time national championship head coach, Dabo Swinney. As a modern-day civil rights leader, he is a close aide to Reverend Jesse Jackson and serves on the Board of Directors of Rainbow PUSH Inc. (Atlanta) and Director of Business Education and Corporate Engagement. He serves on the Board of Fellowship of Christian Athletes (Atlanta Urban) and after the Columbine High School shooting, he founded the National School Safety Advocacy Association. His latest foundations include the Young Entrepreneurship Program (YEP) and the African American Consumer Economic Rights (AACER). He has authored sixteen books that include: *Powerful Prayers That Open Heaven, Capturing and Keeping the Pastor's Heart, Advertising*

118

Principles: How to Effectively Reach African Americans in the 21st Century, Discover a New You: A 21 Day Journey to Uncovering Your Uniqueness, Daily Quotes for Daily Blessings, The Making of a Man, I'm Just Sayin', From My Heart To Yours: Love Letters From A Loving Father, Today's Apostle: Servants of God Leading His People Towards Unity, A Seven Day Prayer Plan for Prosperity, You Have What it Takes, A Marketing Model for Ethnic Consumer Behavior, An Overview of Strategic Healthcare Marketing, The Importance of Subcultural Marketing, A Seven Day Prayer Plan for Peace, and Unshakable Faith.
Apostle Pleasant is a lifetime member of Alpha Phi Alpha Fraternity Inc. He is the loving husband of the pulchritudinous, Kimberly Pleasant and the proud father of three children: Christian, Zion and Nacara.

FINI